A Sufi Coloring Book

A Sufi Coloring Book

A Collection of Sufi Saints and Symbols

Pir Netanel Miles-Yépez

The Inayati-Maimuni Order
Boulder, Colorado
2020

"The old shall be renewed,
and the new shall be made holy."
— Rabbi Avraham Yitzhak Kook

Albion-Andalus, Inc.
P. O. Box 19852
Boulder, CO 80308
www.albionandalus.com

Design and composition by Albion-Andalus Books
Cover design by D.A.M. Cool Graphics
Cover image of "The Illumination of Rabi'a (after Beverly Lanzetta)" by Netanel Miles-Yépez
All illustrations within are copyrighted by Netanel Miles-Yépez.
The illustration of "Zikr Calligraphy" was designed by Sasha Gaynor.

ISBN-13: 978-1-7348750-5-8

Manufactured in the United States of America

For

Evelyn Jones

Founder of the Adult Coloring Movement

Contents

Rabia al-Basri

A Sufi Tea Ceremony

Jalal ad-Din Rumi

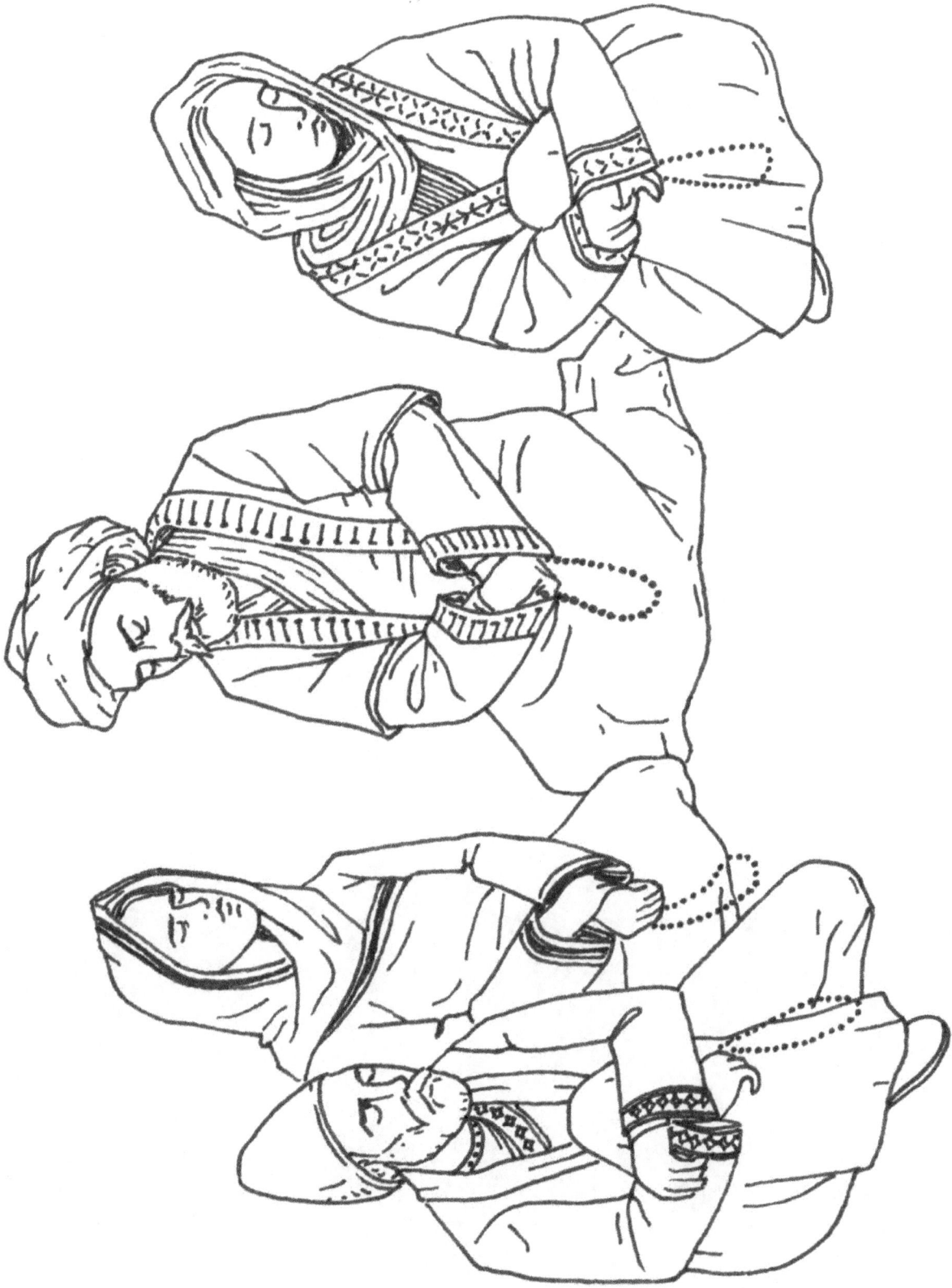

A Sufi Zikr Circle

Jehanara Begum

Leyla and Mejnun

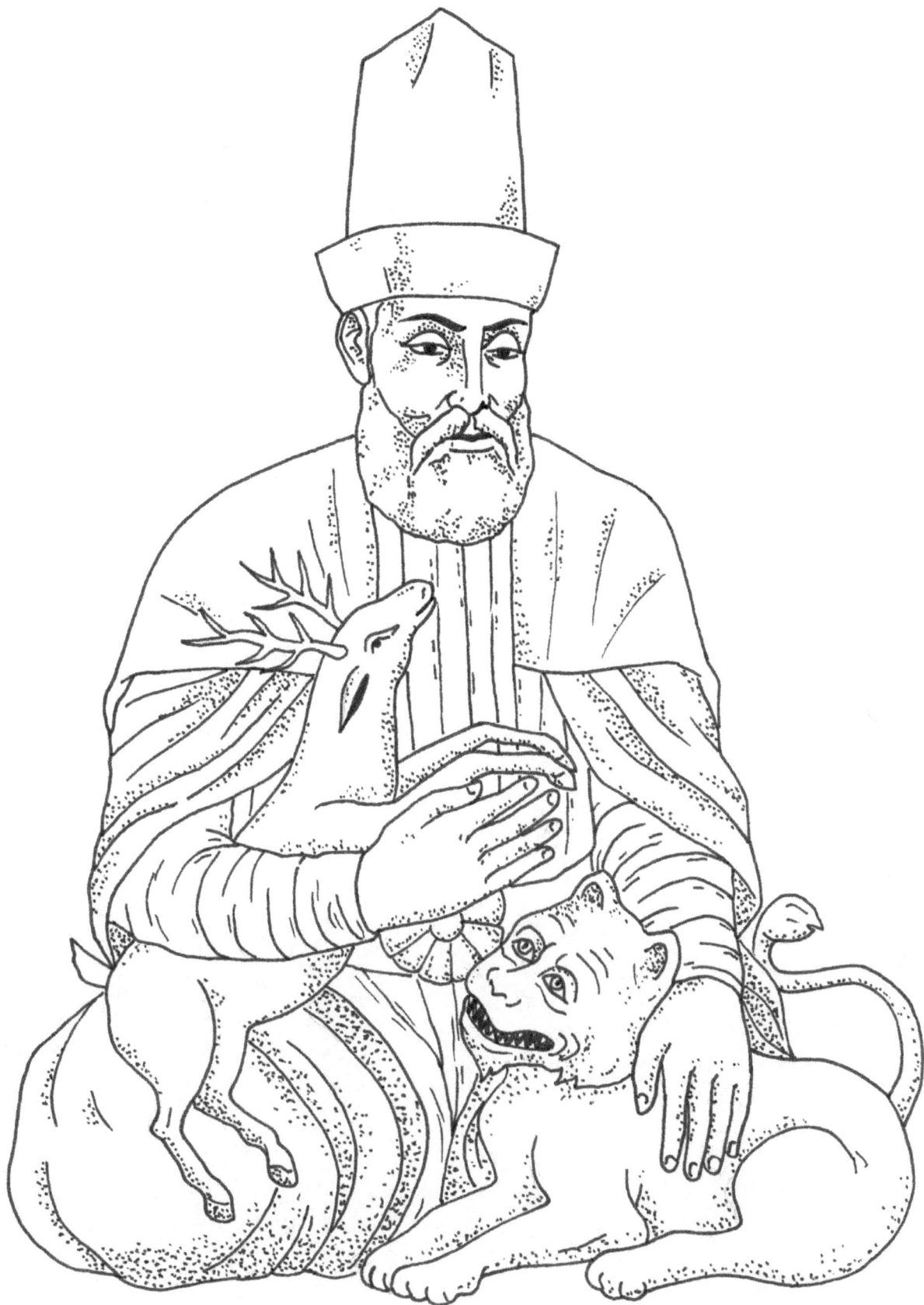

Hadji Bektash Veli

The Sufi Chain

Jehan-Malek Katun

American Heart & Wings

Hazrat Inayat Khan

Shirin and Farhad

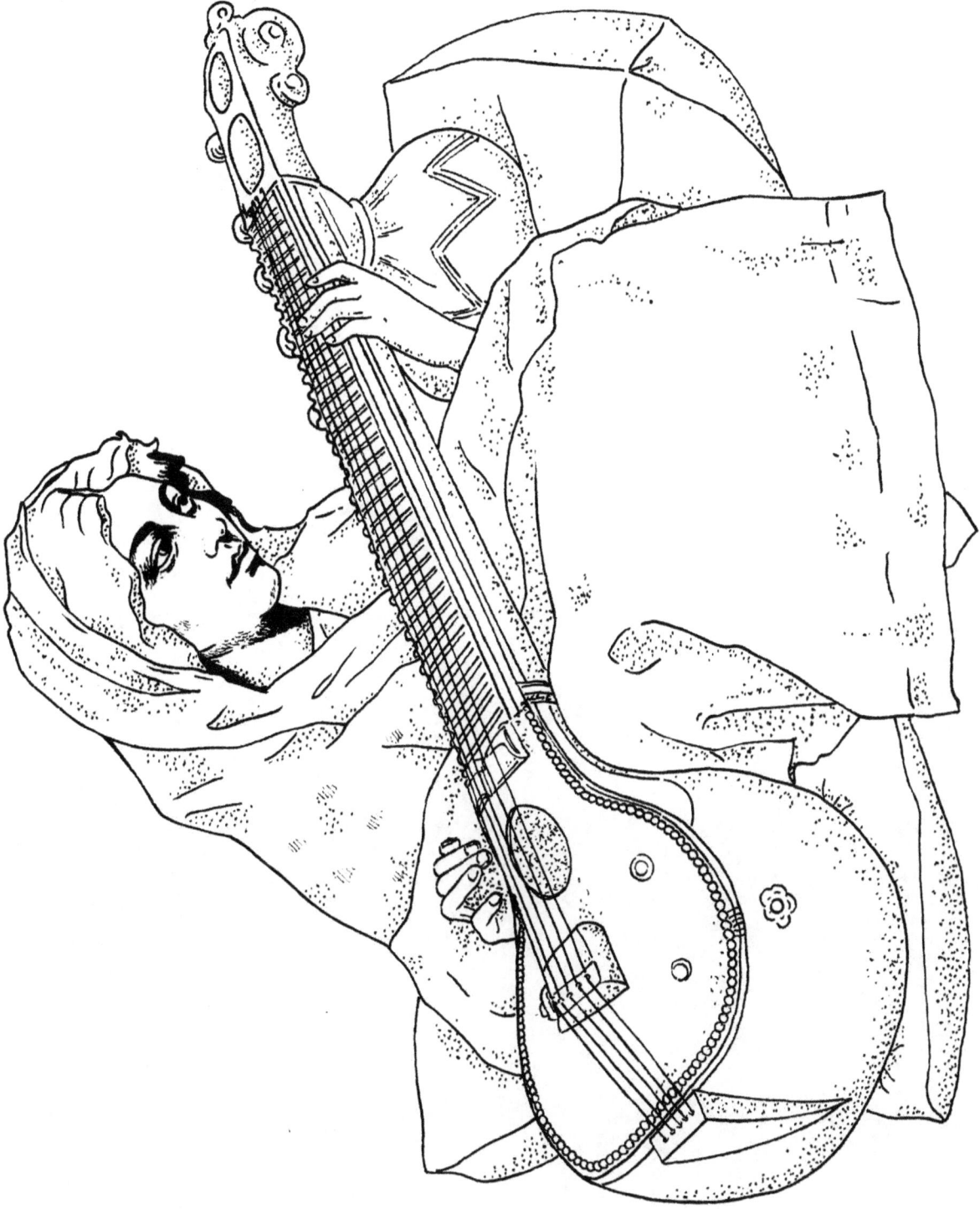

Noor Inayat Khan

Sufi Musicians at Play

Najm ad-Din Kubra

Sufi Authorization.org

Khadija al-Kubra

Muhyiddin ibn 'Arabi

Hazrat Ali

The Drama of Life

Ahmadou Bamba

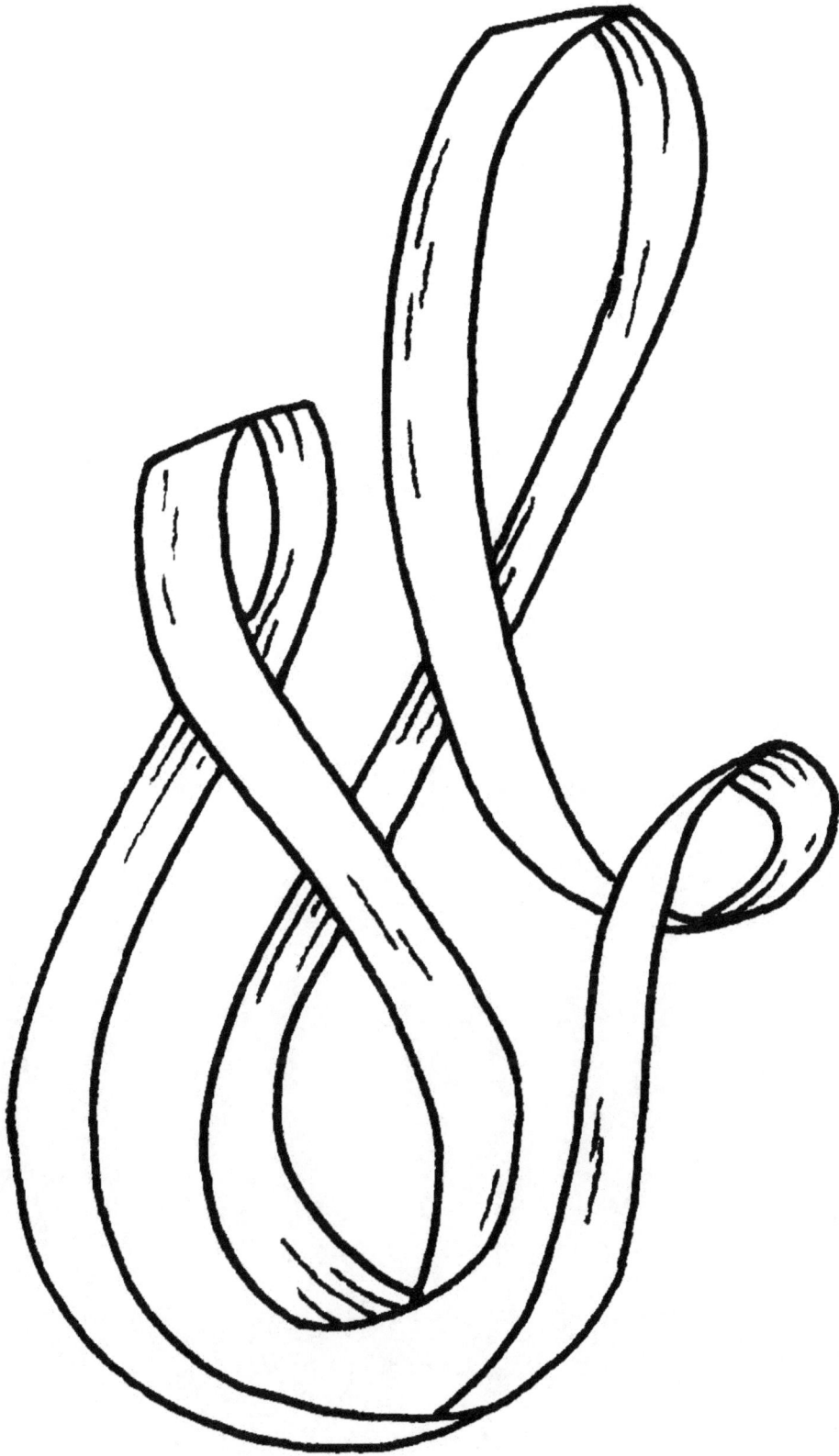

The Calligraphy of Zikr

Coloring Book Guide

Rabia al-Basri

Rabia al-Adawiyya (ca. 714-801) of Basra (in present-day Iraq) was an early Muslim and Sufi saint who was influential in making Sufism a tradition oriented to divine love. This version of her is based on a *retablo* by Beverly Lanzetta called "The Illumination of Rabia."

A Sufi Tea Ceremony

Serving tea or coffee to a guest is an important feature of Sufi *adab* or etiquette.

Jalal ad-Din Rumi

Jalal ad-Din Muhammad Rumi (1207-1273) was a refugee from Balkh, Afghanistan, who made his way with his family to the region of Rum (in present-day Turkey). There he founded the Mevlevi Sufi Order and composed some of the greatest poetry of world literature. This drawing is based on the traditional image of Rumi engaged in *zikr* or 'remembrance' practice.

A Sufi Zikr Circle

A circle *(halqah)* of Sufis engaged in *zikr*, 'remembrance' of God.

Jehanara Begum

Princess *(Shahzadi)* Jehanara (1614-1681) was the eldest daughter of Shah Jehan and his wife, Mumtaz Mahal, for whom he built the famous Taj Mahal. She was a disciple of the Qadiri Sufi master, Mulla Shah, who wished to make her his successor. She was also a devotee of the Khwaja Mu'in ad-Din Chishti, and is buried near the shrines of Chishti Sufi saints. This version of her is based on a painting of Abanindranath Tagore showing her engaged in *zikr* near her father's deathbed.

Layla and Majnun

Often called the "Romeo and Juliet of the Middle-East," Layla and Majnun is a story told in many versions of two historical lovers, Layla and Qays, separated by circumstances, driving Qays to madness. The word, *majnun*, means 'possessed by Jinn,' suggesting that he went mad in his separation from Layla. The most famous telling is that of Nizami. This image depicts the moment the two lovers are re-united.

Hadji Bektash Veli

Hadji Bektash Veli (1209-1271) was a refugee from Nishapur (in present-day Iran) who made his way to Anatolia (in present-day Turkey). A great Sufi saint, Hadji Bektash Veli, the 'pilgrim saint Bektash,' is seen as the founder of the Bektashi Sufi Order and Alevi Sufism. This drawing is based on the traditional image of him.

The Sufi Chain

The lineage of Sufi masters and disciples is called a *silsila*, or 'chain,' each master being seen as a link in that chain.

Jehan-Malek Katun

Jehan-Malek Katun (or Khatun) (ca. 1324-1393) was an Injuid princess from Shiraz (in present-day Iran), among the most skilled and prolific Persian poets of her time. Because of the love themes in her poetry, she is often claimed by Sufis. This drawing is an imagined version of her based on a Persian miniature of a woman.

American Heart & Wings

The heart and wings with a crescent and star within the heart is the symbol of Inayati Sufism, as described by its founder, Hazrat Inayat Khan. This drawing is based on a wood-carved heart and wings hanging at the Abode of the Message in New Lebanon, New York.

Hazrat Inayat Khan

Inayat Khan (1882-1927), called *hazrat* ('the presence'), was a brilliant Indian classical singer and vina player who became a Chishti Sufi master of the Kalimi lineage of "Four School Sufism." At the direction of his master, he came to the United States in 1910, becoming the first Sufi master known to do so. He is the founder of Inayati or Universalist Sufism.

Shirin and Farhad

Two famous lovers in a Persian romance by the poet Nizami. Farhad is the lover who is willing to do anything, even to attempt the impossible, for his beloved, Shirin. This drawing is based on a Persian miniature of the two.

Noor Inayat Khan

Noor-un-Nissa Inayat Khan (1914-1944), the daughter of Hazrat Inayat Khan, was a children's book author and British spy stationed in France during World War II who martyred in a Nazi concentration camp.

Sufi Musicians at Play

Sufi musicians playing the traditional frame drum and reed flute.

Najm ad-Din Kubra

Najm ad-Din Kubra (ca. 1145-1221) was a visionary Sufi saint from Khwarazm (Central Asia) who founded the Kubrawiyya Sufi Order. This drawing is an imagined version of him based on a Persian miniature of a Sufi meditatng in a cave.

Sufi Authorization

A Sufi *shaykh* offering *ijazah,* 'authorization' to be a Sufi teacher.

Khadija al-Kubra

Khadija bint Khuwaylid (ca. 555-619), called *al-kubra*, 'the great,' was a succesful merchant, the first wife of the prophet Muhammad, and the first Muslim convert. Here she is depicted waiting for the return of Prophet Muhammad.

Muhyiddin ibn 'Arabi

Muhyiddin ibn 'Arabi (1165-1240), called the *shaykh al-akbar*, the 'greatest shaykh,' was a Sufi saint and prodigy from Corboba, Spain, who traveled the Muslim world in search of mystical knowledge, and wrote the most sophisticated mystical treatises and poetry of Sufism. He is depicted here riding his horse in the course of his travels.

Hazrat Ali

Ali ibn Abi Talib (601-661) was a younger cousin and son-in-law of the prophet Muhammad. He led a burgeoning Islam as the fourth caliph and, according to many, was the Prophet's principle esoteric or Sufi successor, to whom most Sufi lineages trace themselves. Hazrat Ali was also a famous swordsman and this drawing is based on traditional depictions of him with his sword, Zulfiqar.

The Drama of Life

A drawing depicting the drama of life on a stage. In many mystical traditions, the world is seen as a 'stage' and humanity seen as actors in God's play.

Ahmadou Bamba

Cheikh Ahmadou Bamba Mbacke (1853-1927) was a Senegalese Qadiri Sufi master, leader of a peaceful resistance movement against French colonial rule in Senegal, and the founder of the highly influential Mouridiyya Sufi Order.

The Calligraphy of Zikr

Inspired by the elegant movements of the Inayati-Maimuni *zikr*, a *murid* of the order, Sasha Salika Gaynor, designed this symbol of *zikr*.

Author and Illustrator

Pir Netanel (Mu'in ad-Din) Miles-Yépez is the current head of the Inayati-Maimuni Order of Sufism and a professor in the Department of Religious Studies at Naropa University.

An artist, writer, philosopher, and scholar of comparative religion, Pir Netanel first studied History of Religions at Michigan State University and then Contemplative Religion at the Naropa Institute before pursuing traditional studies and training in both Sufism and Hasidism with his *pir* and *rebbe*, Zalman Schachter-Shalomi, the famous pioneer in interfaith dialogue and comparative mysticism.

Pir Netanel is the author of *In the Teahouse of Experience: Nine Talks on the Path of Sufism* (2020), the translator of *My Love Stands Behind a Wall: A Translation of the Song of Songs and Other Poems* (2015), co-author of *A Heart Afire: Stories and Teachings of the Early Hasidic Masters* (2009), and the editor of various works on InterSpirituality.

Currently, Pir Netanel lives in Boulder, Colorado.

www.ingramcontent.com/pod-product-compliance
Lightning Source LLC
LaVergne TN
LVHW061340060426
835511LV00014B/2033